CAN CULTURES COMMUNICATE?

ℐ

Edward Stewart, *Moderator*

ℐ

Samuel P. Huntington
Laura Nader
Mustafa Safwan
Edward Said

An AEI Round Table held on September 23, 1976
and sponsored by
the American Enterprise Institute for Public Policy Research
Washington, D.C.

This pamphlet contains the edited transcript of
one of a series of AEI forums.
These forums offer a medium for
informal exchanges of ideas on current policy problems
of national and international import.
For the presentation of competing views,
they serve to enhance the prospect
that decisions within our democracy will be based
on a more informed public opinion.
AEI forums are also available on
audio and color-video cassettes.

301.2917

St4c

99848

2ar. 1977

Library of Congress Cataloging in Publication Data

Stewart, Edward C.
 Can cultures communicate?

 (AEI round table ; 22)
 1. Arab countries—Relations (general) with the
United States—Congresses. 2. United States—Relations
(general) with Arab countries—Congresses. 3. Cultural
relations—Congresses. I. Huntington, Samuel P. II.
American Enterprise Institute for Public Policy Research.
III. Title. IV. Series: American Enterprise Institute for
Public Policy Research. AEI round table ; 22.
DS63.2.U5S73   301.29'17'4927073   76-39590
ISBN 0-8447-2093-3

trust between any other groups of individuals—between social classes or generations or, for that matter, between different people in different occupations. It is something which has to be done on an individual basis. Related to that is the need to eliminate from American thinking many stereotypes of Arabs, which are based on ignorance.

PROFESSOR STEWART: You have identified the individual basis of intercultural communication. Dr. Safwan, can you concur with that?

MUSTAFA SAFWAN, psychoanalyst: To start with, I must beg your pardon if my English proves to be hesitating or at times incorrect. As a matter of fact, bad pronunciation may be a handicap or an obstacle to communication between individuals, but, as far as cultures are concerned, one of the main obstacles to communication consists in the fact that man always puts some passion in his relationship to his identity—to his national or social identity. Some of this passion must be renounced to facilitate mutual communication. This point requires longer development which can wait until later.

PROFESSOR STEWART: Are you suggesting that Americans might have some difficulty in handling passion?

DR. SAFWAN: No, I meant all of us, all of us, whatever the group. The very fact of *appartenance*—of belonging—has something gratifying in it, a kind of gratification which must be renounced. I mean, every position implies opposition.

LAURA NADER, Department of Anthropology, University of California, Berkeley: In discussing trust between Arabs and Americans, we must determine which Americans and which Arabs are meant. In the relationship between American oil companies and the heads of Arab states, for example, there has been a great deal of mutual trust, and the two groups have had a long relationship. In the attitudes of Lebanese or Syrian villagers, there is also a tremendous amount of trust because they have relatives in

3

this country who are Americans, and the villagers see this as a natural link. The question might even be turned around to ask why Arabs continue to trust Americans in spite of debacles like the situation in 1967 when the United States condoned Israeli aggression against Jordan, Syria, and Egypt.

We should return to the point Professor Said brought up, which has to do with politicization. Several studies carried out in California analyzed the Arab image used in textbooks in the California schools and in films, cartoons, songs, and other media, made since 1920. These studies indicate that stereotyping is a very important technique in building or sabotaging trust between cultures. If we look at the question through time, we find that in this country from 1920 Arabs were perceived as being good fighters and exotic desert lovers with harem girls, and the rest of it. But, over the past several decades, this image has changed to one of the Arab who is cruel, weak, and decadent. It is probably no surprise that this change should have occurred as interest in the development of the state of Israel began to develop.

To sum up, we should specify exactly which Arabs and which Americans are under discussion, at what point in time, and what the function of the images might be.

PROFESSOR STEWART: You have raised the issue of stereotypes, and how the American perception of Arabs has changed in the last twenty or thirty years. Do we have any examples of Arab perceptions or stereotypes of Americans? Perhaps there is a lack of realism in how people perceive us, compared with how we really are.

PROFESSOR SAID: To compare the two sets of perceptions, again one would have to specify the areas precisely. On the whole, there would be an inequality between the two perceptions for the simple reason that America as a cultural entity to the Arab world is rather different from the reverse. That is to say, the relationship of America to the Arab world has been characterized by strength and by great development. The general Arab image of America and the West has been one of wonder and of some admira-

4

tion, which in the past few decades has, for the most part, soured. There is a long history of cultural attitudes, which could be described as stereotypes, in the West generally, which have filtered into American culture. They are very hard to remove. In time, they may change or be modified, as Professor Nader was saying, but they are not radically changed. Certainly the events of the last two or three years have demonstrated this.

PROFESSOR NADER: I would like to disagree with the pessimism implied there. The image of China changed overnight. We passed from a time when the Chinese could not do anything we considered good, to a time when, to some people, the Chinese cannot do anything bad. The change occurred very dramatically and very rapidly through government leadership. We need not be entirely pessimistic.

PROFESSOR HUNTINGTON: Stereotypes and images can exist on two different levels—we can have stereotypes, first, of individuals and, second, of societies or cultures. Most of our stereotypes are of people in other societies as individuals. As you said, Arabs are viewed as being untrustworthy, weak, cunning, and so forth—all individual characteristics. It is rather striking that what you identified as the recent American stereotype of Arabs is precisely the stereotype which not too long ago Americans had of Jews. The stereotype of Jews has changed, and so has that of Arabs, and you are absolutely correct in saying that these stereotypes can change very quickly as a result of leadership and of images presented in the media. This is because they have little or no basis in reality.

There are, however, real differences, major differences, in cultures and societies in terms of how people relate to each other. Societies differ, people do not. Many years ago, I was a member of a group of ten American scholars and former public officials who went to meet a similar group in Japan. When I arrived in Tokyo, I was met by a Japanese escort, an official from the foreign office. For an incredibly long hour-and-a-half drive into Tokyo from the airport, he wanted to find out who was the

5

leader of our group. We did not have a leader, but this was inconceivable to him. He came back again and again and again trying to find out the hierarchy in the American group of ten.

Ten Americans could get together and cooperate without any defined hierarchy, but in Japan when ten people get together there is a Number One, a Number Two, a Number Three, and so on. The difference is in the way in which individuals organize themselves and perceive their relations to other people in their society.

PROFESSOR STEWART: You are suggesting that there will be differences in society in terms of how people identify with the group. Let me pose a question here. Do any of the differences between "the American identity" and "the Arab identity" block intercultural communications between the two societies? How do the Egyptians feel about that, Dr. Safwan?

DR. SAFWAN: The very idea of stereotypes made me think of an experience I had in Egypt in one of my last visits, two or three years ago. It brings up the question of the effect of American films in building a stereotype of the American image. In Cairo, I saw a film on television about the Korean War, in which an American pilot spread devastation around the country and then got down from his plane and met a child coming from all of this horrid desolation. The pilot was very moved by the spectacle. He took the child in his arms and gave him a piece of chocolate or something like that. It cannot be denied that an image like that distorts one's view of Americans. This image sums up the Egyptian attitude toward Americans. This image of a pilot who can do everything—who can bring evil and good together—is an ideal image, and I think it deforms one's perception. It leads to stereotypes that make authentic or genuine perceptions rather more difficult.

PROFESSOR NADER: Let me give you an example of how stereotypes are being formed today. In discussions of energy in this country, the term *foreign oil* is rarely used.

It is usually *Arab oil*. But, among the seven largest oil producers in the world, Arab countries in fact are absent from the top two, which are Russia and the United States. Arab countries rank only third and seventh. And yet when we talk about why we need such things as nuclear power plants, we do not talk about foreign oil but about Arab oil. This creates a certain stereotype of the power of oil-rich Arab lands that does not conform to reality. Also, in these discussions, it is interesting that most people do not differentiate between *Iranian oil* and *Arab oil*. In fact, they do not understand that the two terms imply different cultures.

PROFESSOR STEWART: You have talked about the stereotypes and how they have changed. If we think of a stereotype as a picture in the mind, does this picture tell more about Arabs or about Americans, particularly as it keeps changing?

PROFESSOR HUNTINGTON: I think it tells something about how Americans perceive their interests, or at least how leading groups in American society see their interest, because these stereotypes do change and do reflect changing interests.

PROFESSOR STEWART: So these changes do not necessarily correlate with changes taking place in Arab society. They are more a commentary on American interests and shifts in those interests.

PROFESSOR HUNTINGTON: There may be some relationship to Arab society—obviously, the Arab world is becoming urbanized and is no longer largely peasant or Bedouin. The change in stereotypes which Professor Nader mentioned at the beginning has some relationship to what is going on in the Arab world, though undoubtedly it is very far from the reality of those changes. But it is frightening how stereotypes can change overnight.

PROFESSOR SAID: For the last two or three decades at least, Arab society has been going through a tremendous number of changes. To talk about Arab society or Arab culture, as we have, is to wipe out important distinctions between the various societies within the Arab world. In many ways, they are quite different from each other, though they do have points in common. Also, we are not taking into account the fact that these societies are constantly in change and that even an Arab in the midst of this change would be hard put to characterize the present stage of his development. The changes are so fast and so revolutionary that the confusion is almost inevitable.

In addition to that, the political atmosphere is highly charged. At no moment that I can remember in the last two decades could relationships between Arab and American societies or cultures be described as peaceful or normal. There has always been some extra dimension which aggravates a situation and makes the sense of change and confusion even greater. That is one reason why people resort to stereotypes—they need something stable to hang on to. Frequently, stereotypes are generated not only out of ignorance but also out of fear.

PROFESSOR STEWART: Professor Huntington mentioned that we need not only to have trust but also to communicate. In connection with your remarks, can we look at some of the problems of cutting across the stereotypes, cutting across the culture differences? In the area of individual or cultural communication between Americans and Arabs, what might be some of the challenges and some of the problems? One of the things that often comes up, for instance, is that Americans tend to note differences between words and actions, and they often see a greater schism between language and behavior in the Arab world than at home. Does this kind of culture difference present a problem in terms of communication?

PROFESSOR SAID: It is curious that many generalizations about this "schism" between words and actions or reality in Arab culture have been made by people who do not know the language. These generalizations about the way Arabs think and the way Arabs speak, and the difference between them, are made on the basis of a few free-floating generalizations about Arab society and Arab mentality. In any other situation, one would openly call this racist. You cannot characterize a culture according to some norm that you impose on the relationships between words and actions and say, "It is perfectly clear that Arabs really never mean what they say"—a popular stereotype.

Words and actions differ in all societies—one must allow for such differences. But to make an arbitrary judgment and say it is greater in Arab societies and less great in Sweden and in the United States is perhaps a rather dangerous form of generalization, which leads to nothing productive.

PROFESSOR NADER: Some people have characterized the student movement of the 1960s in the United States as a rebellion of the young because of the gap between what the American government was saying and what it was doing. The difference between word and act has been the crux of the argument between the so-called student movement and the establishment for the last ten years. Looking at this question cross-culturally, one finds no culture has a monopoly on the gap between word and act. The size of the gap reflects the health of a culture, that is, if the gap between word and act becomes too large for the people of that culture, then there is some trouble there. Similarly, if the gap is too large in an individual, that would indicate a mental health problem.

PROFESSOR HUNTINGTON: This gap is not a phenomenon limited to the 1960s in the American experience. It is something which has been with us virtually from the beginning, particularly in the area of politics. We have set forth an impossible set of political goals and ideals and have talked in rhetorical terms about achieving them. Inevitably, we fall very short and compensate by engaging either in moralism or in cynicism or in hypocrisy, trying to bridge the gap between rhetoric and reality. I would find it difficult to believe that the problem is any greater in the Arab world than it is in the United States.

PROFESSOR STEWART: Can anyone guess the source of

that stereotype about Arabs? Americans often mention this schism though we have acknowledged it is no greater among Arabs than in American society. What is the source of the notion?

PROFESSOR SAID: I think the specific historical source can be found in the general Western perception of what in the nineteenth century was called the Orient. As early as the first part of the nineteenth century, "scientific" generalizations were made on the distinction between what used to be called the Semitic, or Oriental, languages and the Western languages. This was the moment when comparative linguistics was born as a science. From a scientific discussion of a language, such as one of the Semitic languages, generalizations would be made about the kind of mind that would produce that language. A wholesale identification was made of the language with this generalized mentality, and by the middle of the nineteenth century, "the Semitic mentality" was said to be exemplified in its language, which was considered unable to deal with modern—in this case, European—reality.

Such generalizations have been very, very influential. We still frequently hear that Arabic is a rhetorical language, that Arabic is a language of eloquence, that it is in effect a medieval language, and that it cannot deal with modern reality. By imputation, these generalizations are also supposed to apply to the Arab mentality. There is a respectable pedigree for this kind of nonsense, and it *is* nonsense because no linguist today would ever agree with it. But it persists, as Professor Nader was saying. It is to be found in textbooks, not only in high school textbooks but also in college and so-called scientific texts.

DR. SAFWAN: Rather than two mentalities, two functions of speech have been recognized by many anthropologists—Malinowski, for example. Language or speech as a vehicle of communication, an instrument for the communication of practical needs, has been distinguished from expressive speech. The latter kind of speech would be the kind through which one tries, for example, to get recognition in the Hegelian sense. This second function of speech exists in all societies and in some is the more privileged. To put the matter in a brutally simple way, one can use speech either to make money or to make one's own being. It is the second function which is privileged in Arabic, as one feels in talking with Arab people. In America, communication tends to be codified in view of "practical" ends.

PROFESSOR NADER: The mistake people in one culture often make in dealing with another culture is to transfer their functions to the other culture's functions. A political scientist, for example, went to the Middle East to do some research one summer and analyzed Egyptian newspapers. When he came back, he said to me, "But they are all just full of emotions. There is no data in these newspapers." I said, "What makes you think there should be?"

The other comment that I wanted to make, following up on Professor Said's observation, is that the tendency to see one's culture as the most logical, the most beautiful, the most whatever, is a tendency that anthropologists sometimes refer to as ethnocentrism. In the nineteenth century, it was commonplace to look not only at Semitic languages but also at all other non-Western languages of the world and say, "These people are prelogical, they speak like children," or, "They are illogical, they are prescientific." Many labels were used, and, of course, the culture that always came up on top was that of the person doing the analysis. If we went back into Arab history, as we easily can, and read the historians that described early European culture, we would find them doing the same kinds of things and making the same kinds of judgments.

PROFESSOR STEWART: This phenomenon is similar to that of stereotypes, which say a great deal more about the holder of the stereotype than about the other society. Americans often claim, rightly or wrongly, that there is a difference in how the two societies use information and knowledge. In American society, information and knowledge are treated more as a commodity, whereas in Arab societies, they are more often treated as a source of power, something which is accumulated and not necessarily dispensed with the same freedom found in American society. I wonder if we could look at that.

PROFESSOR NADER: As long as someone has previously used the word *racist*, I can use it again. It is just a non-sensical statement, with absolutely no basis. The government studies that are done in this country are all put on shelves after they are done. They are purely for ceremonial purposes, one study after the other. We gather information supposedly to apply to social problems but we never apply it. There is no evidence whatsoever to buttress the statements that you have quoted.

PROFESSOR SAID: It is curious that whatever knowledge there is in the United States of Arab culture is skewed towards classical culture. If a literate American knows anything about Arab civilization, he is likely to know about Ibn Khaldun, Averroes, and people of that sort—that is to say, medieval philosophers, writers, and poets. This person would know little about what is now taking place in the Arab world. This is one of the most striking and peculiar discrepancies between the two cultures, that the relationship is not between one contemporary culture and another contemporary culture, but between a contemporary culture and a classical culture. In the formal study of Arab culture in this country and in the West generally, a great deal of attention is paid either to the classical period or to current sociopolitical or socioeconomic realities, as defined by modern Western political and social scientists. The rather large area of Arab endeavor engaged in ongoing contemporary culture receives no attention whatever, so Americans know nothing about the modern Egyptian novel, for example, or about modern Syrian poetry. A most peculiar sort of time lag exists in the world today.

PROFESSOR STEWART: The other country is always seen out of time, in a sense.

PROFESSOR SAID: Yes, I think this point was made earlier, but it is very important. This is also part of the tradition of looking at the Orient as essentially a classical

12

civilization which got lost long ago. Everything to be found in Arab society appears degenerate somehow, a degraded version of the great classical past. In a curious way, this attitude is reinforced by the belief of many Arabs that their great days of glory are in the past. It is a strange kind of feedback effect, and it is very influential, and regrettable.

PROFESSOR HUNTINGTON: Professor Stewart, I would like to go back to the question you posed earlier concerning knowledge and attitudes towards knowledge and the use of knowledge. One distinctive element in American culture is in its extraordinary emphasis upon spreading knowledge and information, upon exposés, upon publicity. Much of this activity is undoubtedly ceremonial, as Professor Nader suggested, but it is something that distinguishes American culture, even among Western cultures. One does not find in Great Britain this emphasis upon opening up doors, muckraking, exposure, and so forth. In this connection, the media play a much more important role in American culture than in most other Western cultures, and, I would suspect, than in Arab cultures as well.

PROFESSOR STEWART: I am glad you picked up on that point because I too feel different cultures sometimes stress different systems and different functions, as Dr. Safwan was saying. The Japanese, for instance, have a class of words that give nothing but a taste or flavor of the language and have no other meaning. It is language used for an expressive function rather than for the communication of hard information. There are differences among cultures of this kind, as well as political differences and differences in the exchange of information or knowledge.

PROFESSOR SAID: You are making a distinction between information, which you regard as something useful, and other things that are not directly useful but which might also be information. Even when something is said ceremonially in Japanese, it still conveys information. It is a different kind of information, but why should information always be useful?

13

PROFESSOR STEWART: Whether information is an essential exchange of hard facts and data, as we would think, or a direct communication to the individual himself depends upon one's value system.

PROFESSOR SAID: Hard facts are matters of judgment—just say, "That is a hard fact," and it becomes one. It may be a little more complicated than that, perhaps, but in generalizing about cultures it is frequently decided arbitrarily that something is information and something else is not. Arabs are said to spend a great deal of time being "emotional," as if being emotional is not quite as useful or important as conveying hard facts. As many novelists have pointed out, imparting hard facts may be a bad thing after all. There may be too many hard facts around and not enough emotions.

PROFESSOR STEWART: Different values might be placed on expressive or emotional communication and communication that tends to be more "pedestrian," which is used for exchanging facts and figures of different kinds

DR. SAFWAN: Does America have anything like the French Ministry of Information?

PROFESSOR STEWART: I think we have many of those.

DR. SAFWAN: Information is never wholly disinterested as far as a government policy of information may be concerned. Could we say, for example, that there is an Egyptian *citizen* in the sense the term has evolved in the West from its Greek origin? Is there a citizen in Egypt in this sense? There are those who govern and those who are governed, but citizens? I would not dream of trying to answer these questions myself.

PROFESSOR HUNTINGTON: I wish you would engage in some dreaming and answer them for us. They are fascinating questions.

PROFESSOR STEWART: It is often said that in Arab societies people have seen the brilliance of revelation which gives a religious tone to the society and to some of its laws as well. In American society, however, the values of Christianity have become secularized and have lost much of the magnetism of the original revelation. Does this line of thought lead to communication, or is it a block?

PROFESSOR SAID: One of the major presidential candidates certainly does not seem to think that revelation belongs to time past.

PROFESSOR STEWART: He is trying to bring it back.

PROFESSOR SAID: Yes, right. No culture necessarily has a monopoly on revelation. The religious coloration of Arab society has been overstated (I should use the phrase *Arab society* with quotation marks around it because I am not sure which Arab society we are talking about). The same religious coloration can be found in other societies, so the real questions are at what level the religious faith is practiced, whether it influences all aspects of life in society or just some of them, and where, how, and at what times it is practiced.

PROFESSOR HUNTINGTON: If, indeed, Arab society is religiously colored, I would think that would make it more, rather than less, like American society. Religion and religious values and beliefs play a very large role in our culture. Just a little while ago there was a poll of how religious the different peoples of the world were, and, if I remember correctly, Americans ranked next to the top. In terms of belief in God and the formal aspects of religion, Americans always rate very high. A religious character has been very much a part of the American heritage since the origins of the nation, and, despite modernization and secularization, it is still very much with us.

PROFESSOR STEWART: Can we distinguish between a religion that is merely professed and one that governs our daily actions, and then compare American and Arabic societies?

PROFESSOR NADER: This goes back to what you were saying earlier, Professor Said, about seeing the Middle East through classicist glasses. Some fifteen years ago, I went to the Middle East to see if Islamic law, or religious law, was in fact operating in the villages, or had it, being an urban religion, never really penetrated into the villages. In the villages, when we started talking about everyday conflicts and disputes and how they resolve them, lo and behold, I discovered there is no Islamic law operating at all.

The procedures were very pragmatic. The neighborhood councils operated in a way we are trying to invent in certain parts of the United States today. It was an arbitration procedure, sometimes mediated rather than arbitrated, and it was very pragmatic, very secular. I had absolutely no trouble in this village being invited into the mosque. I was a woman, but that did not make any difference, and all of the stereotypes caved in, one after the other. Islamic women, who are often portrayed as being very compressed and repressed and depressed, were much freer in these villages than middle class women I know in Berkeley. They come and go and do pretty much as they want. They often have the power of their lineage to back their position. There is probably less wife beating in this little village in southern Lebanon than there is in Berkeley, California, according to a recent study of wife beating in upper, middle, and lower income groups in Berkeley.

These stereotypes are just that. Instead of trying to explain many things that may not exist, people who want to study the Middle East should find out what is there, what is happening in the area, rather than taking a stereotype and saying, "I wonder why they are so religious?" We do not even know whether they are or not.

PROFESSOR SAID: The study of the Middle East in the West generally, and in this country specifically, has been focused on large, monolithic Platonic concepts such as "Islam," or "the Arabs," as if they had some unchanging existence of their own. As a result, people who profess to know the Middle East engage in an operation like this. They take an immediate political event, or a web of political events—what is taking place in Egypt, for example, or in Syria—and for an ultimate understanding of it, they take a couple of passages from the Koran or from some twelfth-century jurist, and say, "If you really want to understand what is going on, you have to go back to these lines, which are really the secret to it." In looking at the Arab world, this practice is not only tolerated but encouraged, it seems to me.

The equivalent of such folly is to say, "If you really want to understand what is taking place in the Congress on the energy bill, you have to read the New Testament very carefully, and then everything will be clear to you." You may laugh, but this is regularly done in articles by distinguished scholars who say what is going on in the Middle East is really all about Islam.

DR. SAFWAN: What was said about the Middle East village indicates that customs are in the process of changing, but it does not prove that dogma changes. The hold of dogma on the spirit is another matter.

PROFESSOR STEWART: Dr. Safwan, in discussing Arabs and Arab societies, we have made the point a number of times that there may be quite a difference among different segments of it. Would you care to comment on the notion of Arab identity?

DR. SAFWAN: It is simply maddening to hear the insistence in many countries—not only in America or in an Arab country—that the main purpose of education is to affirm that nation's identity or to stress its contribution to civilization. This is a part of an ongoing process of segregation. The main purpose of education should be to create a sense of cultural relativity, which must start in every country, everywhere, and very early in the school program. Something like a history of architecture, for example, should be taught, so a child can know at the age of seven or eight that there is a Moroccan house, an Egyptian house, an Arabic house, a Roman house, an American suburban house. There must be a whole policy of education oriented toward creating a sense of cultural relativity.

17

PROFESSOR STEWART: We are concerned about the problem of communication across cultures, in this case Arab and American. If one were to explore the other's culture for the purpose of enriching one's own, what would Arabs recommend to Americans and what would Americans recommend to Arabs?

PROFESSOR HUNTINGTON: We have identified one major recommendation—to try to dissolve the stereotypes and illusions each culture has of the other. We have had a good deal of discussion here about American stereotypes of Arabs, but what are the Arab stereotypes of Americans and American society? How close are they to reality and how are they changing? The point has been made that stereotypes can be easily managed and can change frequently. I suspect that many Arab stereotypes of Americans have been at least as unfavorable as American stereotypes of Arabs, and I would hope that there are institutions at work in the Arab world to change those, too.

PROFESSOR SAID: We have been rather unfair, or at least uneven, in this discussion by focusing on American or Western stereotypes of Arabs and we have not really talked about the other thing. So far as I know, there is no formal institution in the Arab world devoted to the study of the United States. I know of none to be found in any university. There are no departments of American studies, as there are departments of Middle East studies in this country. As for Arab stereotypes of Americans, they may not be as pernicious as American stereotypes of Arabs—or perhaps they are—but they are certainly funnier.

PROFESSOR HUNTINGTON: Americans may be funnier people.

PROFESSOR SAID: Yes, perhaps that is the reason. That means that the stereotypes are more correct. Considering the intimacy and urgency of relationships between the Arab world and the United States, there is an extraordinary lack of Arab purpose in trying to find out more about the United States in any systematic way. There are people who write

18

impressions, travel diaries, and things of that sort, but there are no collective and formalized efforts to be found. Conversely, the means of finding out more about Arabic culture here are very humble, given the politicized and rather nasty atmosphere, which we have pretended is just not there. The solution is to read more. One has to be more involved with literature.

PROFESSOR NADER: I would say that we ought to specify what we can learn from each other—and this is a plea for specificity. If we asked an Arab "What could you teach an American?" he might say "hospitality." Then the southern American would say, "What do you mean? Have you forgotten about southern hospitality?" If we ask an American "What could you teach the Arabs?" he might say "efficiency." Then we look at how the nomads utilize the most forlorn desert areas of the world and think, "Can we really teach the nomads how to utilize that area more efficiently?"

In the area of law, the Arabs can teach us something about situationalism and how to decide cases on a less than zero-sum-game basis, and more on a give-a-little, get-a-little basis. Arabs have something to teach us about cuisine, about art, about expression. We could also turn it around and say the United States might teach the Middle East something about freedom of political speech. The Middle East might trade us some of their shame, and we could give them some of our guilt culture. That would certainly relieve a lot of American working women, I must say.

What are the kinds of things we might cooperate on? Let's take a look at solar technology. They have lots of sun, and some money, and we have a lot of know-how. That would be a good way to get both cultures working together.

PROFESSOR STEWART: Our panelists have been trying to explore some of the aspects of inter-cultural communication. It is our custom as Americans to consider cultural differences as impediments to communication, but I sense from what our panelists have said that perhaps we should discard that idea. We can perceive culture differences as human resources and learn to use them and enrich our lives thereby. The panelists are now open to questions from the audience.

PETER BECHTOLD, Foreign Service Institute: I listened with great interest and with growing disbelief to some of the comments of the panelists. On one hand we were told that specialists are trying to interpret contemporary events by quoting medieval manuscripts and the Koran. I have spent more than fifteen years in close contact with specialists on Arab affairs, both in government and in academia, and in no more than 1 percent of the cases was that true. In fact, there is a growing familiarity, awareness, and understanding on the part of American audiences toward Arab culture. This brings me to another point. The panelists try to suggest that the stereotypes are bad stereotypes, and perhaps they are. But it has been my experience, and I think that of most of us here, that the effective action of an American in the Arab world depends to a very great degree on the extent to which he does not act like an American. Cultural differences can be bridged, but it would be wrong to underestimate them in terms of speech, in terms of daily behavior, in terms of businesslike conduct versus sociability, et cetera. As a result of the growing awareness of Americans and the growing number of centers of Middle Eastern studies, cultural communication has improved tremendously. I do not see the problems that have been mentioned here.

PROFESSOR NADER: There is certainly a difference between what is written about the Middle East and practical experience with the Middle East, and you are talking about practical experience. In a way, practical experience is quite a bit ahead of academic analyses of the Middle East, but it is from the written material that people without firsthand experience learn about the Middle East. In this country, most people's experience with the Middle East is second-hand experience.

PATRICK VISCUSO, Georgetown University: I am very puzzled by your views on Islam, Dr. Nader. Are you saying that Islam now plays a negligible role in Arab culture and its relations to other cultures, and, if so, is this due to westernization?

PROFESSOR NADER: No, I am not saying that Islam plays a negligible role. I am saying that it is something that needs to be studied. I asked one question, and I spent a summer trying to answer it. The question was, Has Islamic law penetrated into Islamic villages? I studied a Shi'ite Moslem village, a Sunnite village, and then a mixed Christian-Shi'ite village. In settling disputes, all of the villages do some things in common that have nothing to do with their religions. It was a very specific area.

MR. VISCUSO: I assume this was in Lebanon. There is a difference, you realize, between Lebanon and Saudi Arabia, for instance.

PROFESSOR NADER: Absolutely. That is the point.

KAMAL BOULLATA, artist, Washington, D.C.: No culture exists in a vacuum. Dr. Said mentioned that there is mis-communication, perhaps, between America and the Arab world because of the very highly politicized atmosphere. Why was this very important point of politicization never developed by the panel? Individualism in America is a result of a political system. Despotism in the Arab world is a result of political systems. Could anybody respond, please?

PROFESSOR HUNTINGTON: There are two different issues involved in what this gentleman has suggested. One is the differences in political systems between Arab societies and the United States, which nobody on the panel mentioned, perhaps because it is so obvious.

There is the second issue of the nature of Arab-American relations and the extent to which they are politicized, as they clearly are. There is the suggestion made by the questioner that because these relations are heavily politicized, this leads to a miscommunication or a misperception, or great difficulties of perception. That may be true in some respects, but I do not think it necessarily has to be the case. It is quite possible for American political leaders and politicians to deal effectively with Arab political leaders and politicians. One has only to look at Edward Sheehan's descriptions of the negotiations our secretary of state had with Arabs and Israelis to see that his biggest communication problems were in communicating with the Israelis, not the Arabs, at least by Sheehan's account. Politicization is going to exist and it need not be viewed as abnormal or bad in relations between people.

PROFESSOR SAID: When I raised the question at the outset, I did not mean to suggest that politicization was necessarily bad, but that, in intercultural relations, it had a narrowing effect and made the relationships between cultures rather less than broad. Political pressures have made relationships between cultures very specialized and have tended to focus attention on a few matters and to misconstrue certain realities—not only political but also cultural realities. When the atmosphere is politicized and narrowed, certain things are selected for attention and others are not.

The Arabs basically represent two things to America. On the one hand, they are oil producers, and, on the other, they are anti-Israeli. Nearly everything that stands for Arab culture can be placed, more or less, under one of those two headings, and that fact tends to focus the issue a great deal.

There is also a third element—the relationship between the United States and the Arab world is an unequal one. It is unequal because of tradition, because of power, and to a certain extent because of history. The Arab world until very recently was part of the colonial world, and this obviously colors its relationships with the United States. The United States has taken too little account—culturally, politically, or otherwise—of the fact that the Arab world is in a state of extremely turbulent change, a change directly related to its colonial and imperial past.

DONALD TANNENBAUM, Gettysburg College: I heard a remark about trying to understand the United States Congress by understanding the Bible. My personal point of view is that it might not be a bad approach. I also think it would be well to investigate the villages of the United States to understand what Congress is about. This suggests that there are several levels of culture, perhaps, in very simple terms a micro level and a macro level, with many interlevels between. Would any of the panelists care to state a preference for beginning at one level rather than another in approaching the problem of communication between cultures. Should we communicate macro-cultural concepts or micro-cultural concepts if both are not possible simultaneously?

PROFESSOR NADER: The American Friends Service Committee thinks that there ought to be more communication at the micro level, so they have set up programs whereby young people can go and live in small communities around the world. In the Middle East, the United States has operated largely on the macro level, with the exception of a few things like the Peace Corps.

In regard to American villages, I would like to see Middle Easterners study this country just as we study other countries. There are very few studies of American culture by foreigners. That is one reason why Tocqueville is studied and quoted so often. No Middle Eastern or Arab anthropologist has ever made a study of an American village, city, or town, or Congress, or anything else. Anthropologically, we probably have the most unstudied culture in the world. When it is studied, we will begin to get an interchange of information at the micro level, and I think that is important.

PHILIP N. MARCUS, National Endowment for the Humanities: I would like to ask Mr. Safwan a question to follow up on the discussion about identity. I would like to ask it by referring to two examples. Could an Egyptian psychoanalyst provide treatment for a Syrian? Could an American psychoanalyst provide treatment for an Arab?

DR. SAFWAN: My own experience has been in France, with patients coming from every social class, workers as well as the bourgeoisie. I practiced in Egypt for some few years and had a clientele mainly of university people, but I also treated some with moderate education. I even had some women with no education at all.

The only differences that I found were differences in customs, in manners, or in beliefs. Differences in cultural beliefs and habits may fortify some rationalization or may make their undoing more difficult, but as far as the final issues are concerned—the ultimate bases of neurosis, for example, or positional neuroses or hysteria—they are absolutely the same in every culture. To give a brief answer, the differences I encountered in my practice may influence the modulation of the work but not the sense of it.

PROFESSOR NADER: Are you saying that cultural relativity does not apply to analysis?

DR. SAFWAN: I would circumscribe its effect in that it modulates the work differently. In this context, I would like to hear a definition of *self*. I know it is the current notion in psychiatry and cultural anthropology, but I have never heard an acceptable definition of it.

MUHAMMAD ABDUL RAUF, the Islamic Center in Washington: It seems that the experience of Dr. Nader in some of the Moslem villages and with some Moslem women has led to a suggestion of the alienation of Islamic law. We seem to have certain stereotypes about Islamic law itself and about the Islamic spirit, but I believe that the liberty enjoyed by Moslem women and their pragmatic way of handling daily affairs agree with the spirit of Islamic law and the teaching of Islam itself. That is just an observation, not a question.

FREDERIC CADORA, Ohio State University: My question is related to the one preceding the last. Can an Arab psychoanalyst analyze an American, and can an American psychoanalyst analyze an Arab? Can the differences or the problems highlight differences in their cultural problems?

DR. SAFWAN: Can you make an analysis in a foreign language? I myself made analyses with French-speaking persons, even though some of them were American, because they spoke French perfectly. Knowing French myself, there was absolutely no difficulty. In Egypt, an analysis can be undertaken only with a thorough knowledge of the language of the patient.

PROFESSOR SAID: One matter we have not touched at all is the development since World War II, and particularly in the last decade, of a common language between American, or Western, intellectuals and Arab intellectuals. Intercultural communication, which we have been discussing on the popular level, has also become much more possible on another level, the level of literacy, partly because of the media, partly because communication is mechanically much more simple and direct, and partly because of certain common educational experiences. Most Arab intellectuals today are educated, if not in the West, then in a sense by the West. There is a common vocabulary in which the concepts of psychoanalysis, for example, or the notions of political economy and Marxism can be assumed to be understood, albeit in different ways, among Arabs and Americans. That is something we have not discussed but it should be emphasized.

PROFESSOR STEWART: There may be—exaggerating a bit—a kind of universal intellectual culture, which has nothing to do with "culture" culture.

PROFESSOR SAID: Right, or with universalizing that tends to diminish the differences between cultures.

EMILE A. NAKHLEH, Mt. St. Mary's College: Arab-American intellectuals, particularly academics, face a special problem in their attempt to correct some of the stereotypes concerning Arab political society. This problem is particularly acute when questions of individual freedom and liberty are raised. Most Arab-American academics believe that individual freedom and individual liberty are absent in Arab political societies and that totalitarianism is the hallmark of most Arab regimes. I have faced this problem, and I would like Dr. Said to comment on this dilemma in which most of us find ourselves.

PROFESSOR SAID: It is certainly true that Arab-Americans put near the top of their list the question of political freedom and freedom of speech, which they find lacking in their countries of origin or in the Middle East generally. This has not prevented them from making their opinions known. I do not want to sound as if we are patting ourselves on the back, but we have raised the issue, and the issue is an important one for us. As you say, the issue does present problems, because an Arab-American in America is obviously very conscious not only of his Arab identity but also of his existence in a political culture that is largely hostile to him. He is rather torn by a national loyalty to do something about the Arab position on the one hand, and, on the other, he must be honest enough to see that the freedom of the individual is considerably curtailed in Arab society and does not seem to be improving much.

MOHAMMAD HAKKI, Embassy of Egypt, Washington, D.C.: The question should not be whether an American can analyze an Arab or whether an Arab can analyze an American, but rather could Dr. Kissinger, for instance, be psychoanalyzed by an Arab doctor and allow that fact to be published? In other words, are we overcoming the basic bias?

DR. SAFWAN: If he is neurotic, and if he asks us for it, yes, we can analyze him. In answering the other question, I thought the idea of an Arab or an American analyst ill-expressed. It would be better to say an Arabic-speaking analyst or an English-speaking analyst.

MR. HAKKI: My question is, Are we overcoming the basic institutionalized bias? Not long ago there was a long article in the *New York Times Sunday Magazine* about the Arabists in the State Department, as if they were suspect, as if they were somehow anti-Semitic. Are we approaching the time in America when it is no longer suspect to be an Arabist or when being a specialist in Arab affairs is not somehow held against a person in the media or in the publishing world or in other institutions?

PROFESSOR SAID: There is an essay by the famous man of letters—perhaps the most famous one of this century—Edmund Wilson, in a book he wrote in the fifties, *Red, Black, Blond, and Olive*, which deals with his visits in Haiti, the Soviet Union, and Israel. In that book, he says that it is more or less natural for any American, by virtue of his cultural background and training, to hold Arabs and Arab civilizations in contempt. This contempt is a powerful strain, it seems to me, and it has become exacerbated by the political atmosphere. One could use the word *Arab* or *Arabist* as an insult, or as a kind of political designation that is quite suspect. It is equivalent, for example, to *anti-Semitic*, or *fascist*. We are a long way from escaping from that, and I am not sure that the Arabs are entirely blameless in this respect. The anti-Arab feeling is still very much there.

PROFESSOR HUNTINGTON: This is a general problem in relations between Americans and other countries, and not something peculiar to Arab-American relations. The people in the United States who have special relationships or special interests with particular foreign countries are often viewed with suspicion. Almost everybody in the United States concerned in any way with foreign affairs has some sort of special relationship, even in a professional sense. The specialists in Latin America are often viewed by others as overrepresenting the interests of Latin America in American society and culture. We also have people with ethnic ties, obviously, to other parts of the world, though we have fewer with ties to the Arab world than to other regions. In most cases, the ethnic and the professional groups try to influence American policy according to their special interests, and they often succeed.

PROFESSOR NADER: When there are stereotypes about other cultures, such as Mexican culture, for example, or Chicano culture in this country, there are also enough counter examples so that people say, "But some of my best friends are Chicanos, and they are educated." The Arab-American population, however, is very tiny, and so people learn about Arab culture secondhand, for the most part. Also, there is an interest group in this country that is doing a negative P.R. job on the Middle East, and there is nothing to counter it. That is why the Arab-American case is different from the Chicano case or even from the Japanese Americans, who tend to be clustered in one place.

PROFESSOR SAID: I think the case of the Arab in this culture differs from any other foreign or non-American culture group. Prominent Americans take positions on questions relating to South Africa or Chile or other foreign political issues, but none of those Americans takes a similar position in favor of the Arabs. That is a very dramatic and important distinction. A favorable position may be taken on most issues, generally speaking, but not in regard to the Arab world. It would be hard for any of us here to identify an Arab partisan.

PROFESSOR HUNTINGTON: Oh, come on, the chairman of the Senate Foreign Relations Committee for ten or twelve years was prominently identified as an Arab partisan, and with good reason. There is nothing wrong with that.

K. I. SEMAAN, State University of New York at Binghamton: In Malta last year I witnessed firsthand intercultural communication between some of my American students and Libyan students. Without going into any descriptions, since I recorded them and am in the process of formulating my own conclusions, I want to address a question to the panel. Can government policy bring about intercultural communication on the personal level?

DR. SAFWAN: Through education, maybe. The only change I see will come through education policy.

PROFESSOR NADER: Again, China is an example of a dramatic change in the relations not only between governments but also between people on a personal level. Now scientists have personal exchanges, and that is the beginning of further communication.

MR. SEMAAN: I should like to add that some of my American students did strike up good friendships with Libyan students. The Americans were shocked to find the Libyans the exact opposite of what they had expected, based on their government's descriptions of the leader of the Libyan government and on what they had read in the newspapers and elsewhere.

PROFESSOR HUNTINGTON: There have been many U.S. policies and programs designed precisely to encourage communications at the personal level—including the Fulbright programs and the Peace Corps and a variety of others. I do not know how successful they have been, but personal communication has been uppermost, I would think, in the minds of American officials.

PETER S. TANOUS, Peter S. Tanous Co., Inc.: As an American businessman I travel quite a bit in the Middle East. One area that you all have neglected is a micro approach on cultural communications. In my trips to the Middle East, for example, I am absolutely amazed at the number of people I meet who have been educated in the United States and who continue to make trips to the United States. They bring the American culture back to their individual countries.

PROFESSOR NADER: That is much more common than the reverse. There are Americans who were educated at the American University in Beirut and Cairo, but the tourism in the area does not even begin to balance Arab tourism here, so I think you are probably right. There are lots of micro communication patterns opened up by these people but it goes one way mainly.

DAVID DAVIES, American Friends of the Middle East: I taught for three years in Saudi Arabia and I would like to tell a little story to answer Professor Stewart's question, "Do cultural differences cause breakdown in communication?" I was driving with one of my students, and I asked him, "Where are you from?"—four very simple English words. I knew he knew them because I had taught them to him. He named a little village about 500 kilometers away from Riyadh, and I said, "Oh, when did you come to Riyadh?" He looked at me in a very puzzled way, and I said, "If you are from that village, when did you come to Riyadh?" He said, "Oh, I have always lived here in Riyadh." And I said, "But you are from there." He said, "Oh, my grandfather was from there." So the answer first is, yes, cultural differences can create a barrier to communication. But, in following up and discovering that it was his tribal affiliation that brought on his answer, I learned a lot about his culture. The answer then is, yes, cultural differences can be a great source of information and a great thing to build on for mutual instruction.

PROFESSOR STEWART: Thank you. I do think there has been a tendency on the part of the panel to pass over differences, and I have sensed in the audience an effort to go back to them. Do we have any other questions?

MICHAEL D. SHAFER, Department of State, Bureau of Education and Cultural Affairs: I am intrigued by the way this entire discussion has gone around the question of Islam. One thing that defines American culture is that it, like Europe, lives on the assumption that this is the world that has followed Eden. We live in a fallen world, and I suspect that is one of the reasons we feel so uncomfortable with one of our presidential candidates' statements about being born again.

It seems to me that the Moslem-Arab world is built on exactly the opposite premise—that this is, to borrow an expression from a Christian, the city of God, the world of God. Within the Arab world itself, one of the most important intellectual discussions at present is the reconciliation of the incredible tradition of Islam with the culture brought in by 200 years of European colonization. Would anybody care to comment on the possibilities for conflict and misunderstanding between the United States, as a representative of the European culture, and the Arab-Islamic culture, which is so close to God in some ways?

PROFESSOR SAID: That is a very complicated and subtle question. Earlier, I brought up the question of Islam and how it is used to interpret the Middle East. What I had in mind simply was a tendency among authorities in the field, whose training suggests a rather special relationship with Islam based on classical Islam. The tendency of such commentators is to treat Islam reductively, as if to say Islam is simply this, a very simple thing. And they imply that a very complex phenomenon can be understood by reducing it to a very simple thing, which is Islam.

It is certainly true that there is a widespread and fascinating debate taking place in many places in the Middle East about the relationship between Islam and modernity. But the fact is that these changes are taking place, and they can not be easily reduced to a simple either/or question of whether one should reject Islam or accept it. It is not that simple because human societies do not work that way.

Without wishing to pose as an authority on the subject, I think it is dangerous to be too simplistic and say that, since they are Islamic, *this* is what they are and *that* attitude has prevailed.

PROFESSOR NADER: We need to know more about Islamic behavior. There is a lot written about Islamic thought, but there is a lot less written about the behavior associated with that thought.

31

THOMAS G. ROULETTE, consulting psychologist: In the decade or so that I have worked at the American-Arab interface, I have perceived a prime dilemma in the Arab world over how to get both feet into the twentieth century and gain all of its technology without giving up Arab and Islamic cultural traditions, and this seems to be quite a problem. I wonder if some of our cultural experts could comment on whether they see this as a problem and how they would bet on the resolution of this dilemma.

PROFESSOR HUNTINGTON: As the person on this panel who has the least knowledge of and least involvement with Arab culture, I am perhaps least qualified to answer that question. I can say, however, that other cultures have wrestled with the same problem and, in many cases, have come up with successful answers to it. Japan has modernized with spectacular success, and yet it has been able to preserve many of the traditional Japanese ways of thought and of doing things.

Other cultures, including the Chinese, are in the process of modernization and yet seem to be able to establish a compromise between modern values and ways of behavior on the one hand and those of their traditional culture on the other.

PROFESSOR NADER: This is a ubiquitous problem—how to have your cake and eat it too. The problem is more serious and more difficult to solve everywhere in the world today for one simple reason—increasing centralization. As long as the strength of multinational corporations increases, they will peddle not only items but also systems, and when systems are being peddled, it is not possible to pick and choose only what is wanted. Either the whole basket of fruit must be accepted or none at all. This is the problem being faced not only by the Middle East but worldwide. It is not the same problem that was faced a hundred years ago. It is of a different magnitude, and it has to do with the increasing centralization of economic interests in the world.

PROFESSOR SAID: Is that the particular problem of the Middle East, of the Arab cultures?

PROFESSOR NADER: Yes, that is right.

PROFESSOR SAID: That was what the question seemed to have expressed, but that may not necessarily be the case. It is a problem, but there may be other more pressing problems, which cannot be dealt with under the title of modernization.

MR. ROULETTE: I am not certain that modernization actually is a problem, but it is perceived and discussed in the Middle East as a problem.

PROFESSOR NADER: The problem often is that importing the technology creates the problem. The Arabs gave Stanford Research Institute a half-million-dollar contract and said, "Tell us how Americans take care of their old people so we can take care of our older people." But the Arabs had never had a problem with aging or with taking care of old people until they gave this contract to SRI. Now the Saudi Arabians are going to have old-age homes, probably scattered throughout the desert in oases and other delightful places.

PROFESSOR STEWART: Time flows on and eventually engulfs us all. Before we run out of time, let me thank the panelists for their contributions, and the audience for its penetrating questions and comments Thank you. [Applause.]